PRENTICE HALL

UNITED STATES HISTORY

All-in-One Teaching Resources

World War II (1941–1945)

PEARSON

Prentice
Hall

Upper Saddle River, New Jersey
Boston, Massachusetts

Acknowledgements

Page 21: Excerpt from NIGHT by Elie Wiesel, translated by Marion Wiesel. Translation copyright © 2006 by Marion Wiesel. Reprinted by permission of Hill and Wang, a division of Farrar, Straus and Giroux, LLC.

NOTE: Every effort has been made to locate the copyright owner of material reprinted in this book. Omissions brought to our attention will be corrected in subsequent editions.

Upper Saddle River, New Jersey
Boston, Massachusetts

ISBN 0-13-203689-4

1 2 3 4 5 6 7 8 9 10   10 09 08 07 06

Name _____ Class _____ Date _____

Dear Family,

Over the coming weeks, our United States history class will be reading a chapter called World War II. The following information will give you some background to the content your student will be studying.

The entrance of the United States into World War II enabled the Allies to advance against Germany and Italy in Europe and Japan in the Pacific. In 1943, the Allies had neutralized German U-boats and the Soviet Union had successfully turned back the German advance at Stalingrad. Allied bombers began raids on Germany in order to halt German manufacturing and demoralize the nation. The United States made great sacrifices and organized its manufacturing at home in order to bolster the Allies' efforts. Women and African Americans gained employment at war factories. However, the civil liberties of Asian Americans were compromised as they were forced into camps for fear that they might be spies for the Axis Powers. In Germany, Adolf Hitler imprisoned millions of Jews in concentration camps during the Holocaust. The Nazi party persecuted Jews and transported them to the camps in which millions were executed. It was not until the German surrender and the liberation of the camps that the world realized the extent of Hitler's programs.

In June 1943, the Allies launched the largest military operation in history as they landed on the beaches of Normandy in northern France, beginning the advance of the Allies in Europe. Along with the Soviets from the east, American and British soldiers fought their way towards Berlin, finally defeating the Germans in June 1945. In the Pacific, Allied forces faced strong opposition from the Japanese, but used a strategy called island hopping. In 1945, President Harry S. Truman decided that the atomic bomb should be dropped on the Japanese cities of Hiroshima and Nagasaki in order to end the war swiftly. Following the end of the war, the world changed significantly. Britain and the United States sought to spread democracy, and the Soviet Union wanted to create communist states in Eastern Europe. In the years following the war, the United States and the Soviet Union emerged as superpowers that dominated global politics. The United Nations was created as an international organization that would promote peace and humanitarian efforts around the world. The United States emerged from World War II as perhaps the strongest nation in the world and would experience tremendous prosperity in the following years.

In the weeks ahead, your student may wish to share what he or she is learning with you. Please participate in your child's educational experience through discussion and involvement.

Sincerely,

SEGUNDA GUERRA MUNDIAL
Carta para el hogar

Estimada familia,

En las próximas semanas, nuestra clase de historia de Estados Unidos va a leer un capítulo llamado "Segunda Guerra Mundial". La siguiente información le dará a usted algunos conocimientos sobre el tema que su estudiante va a estudiar.

La entrada de Estados Unidos en la Segunda Guerra Mundial permitió a los Aliados avanzar contra Alemania e Italia en Europa y contra Japón en el Pacífico. En 1943, los Aliados habían neutralizado los submarinos alemanes y la Unión Soviética había hecho retroceder el avance alemán en Stalingrado. Comenzaron los bombardeos Aliados en Alemania para detener la manufactura alemana y para desmoralizar a la nación. Estados Unidos hizo grandes sacrificios y organizó su manufactura para apoyar el esfuerzo de los Aliados. Las mujeres y los africano-americanos fueron empleados en fábricas de armamentos. Sin embargo, las libertades civiles de los asiático-americanos se vieron comprometidas cuando fueron forzados a vivir en campamentos por miedo a que fueran espías para los Ejes del Mal. En Alemania, Adolf Hitler encarceló a millones de judíos en campos de concentración durante el holocausto. El partido Nazi persiguió a los judíos y los envió a campos de concentración en los cuales millones fueron ejecutados. No fue sino hasta la rendición de Alemania y la liberación de los campos de concentración que el mundo se dio cuenta de la magnitud de los programas de Hitler.

En junio de 1943, los Aliados lanzaron la mayor operación militar de la historia cuando desembarcaron en las playas de Normandía en el norte de Francia, lo que dio inicio a avance de los Aliados en Europa. Junto a los soviéticos desde el este. Los soldados estadounidenses y británicos lucharon hasta llegar a Berlín, para finalmente derrotar a los Alemanes en junio de 1945. En el Pacífico, las fuerzas aliadas enfrentaron una dura resistencia de los japoneses, pero usaron una estrategia llamada de isla en isla. En 1945, el presidente Harry S. Truman decidió que se debía lanzar la bomba atómica sobre las ciudades japonesas de Hiroshima y Nagasaki para terminar la guerra rápidamente. Luego del final de la guerra, el mundo cambió radicalmente. Gran Bretaña y Estados Unidos buscaron diseminar la democracia y la Unión Soviética quería crear estados comunistas en Europa del Este. En los años posteriores a la guerra, Estados Unidos y la Unión Soviética emergieron como superpotencias que dominaban la política mundial. Se creó las Naciones Unidas como una organización internacional que promoviera la paz y los esfuerzos humanitarios en el mundo. Estados Unidos emergió de la Segunda Guerra Mundial, quizás como la nación más poderosa del mundo y experimentó una gran prosperidad en los años siguientes.

En las próximas semanas, es posible que su estudiante quiera compartir con usted lo que ha aprendido. Por favor participe en la experiencia educativa de su hijo o hija a través de conversaciones e involucrándose en su trabajo.

Atentamente,

WORLD WAR II 1941–1945

1. The Allies Turn the Tide

Pacing
2 periods
1 block

L1	Special Needs
L2	Basic to Average
L3	All Students
L4	Average to Advanced

Section Objectives

■ Analyze the response for and impact of the Allies' "Europe First" strategy.

■ Explain why the battles of Stalingrad and Midway were major turning points in the war.

■ Discuss how the Allies put increasing pressure on the Axis in North Africa and Europe.

Terms and People • Dwight Eisenhower • George S. Patton, Jr. • unconditional surrender • saturation bombing • strategic bombing • Tuskegee Airmen • Chester Nimitz • Battle of Midway

Focus Question: How did the Allies turn the tide against the Axis?

PREPARE TO READ

Build Background Knowledge
Preview the section, and remind students that Europe had already been at war for two years when Japan attacked the United States in 1941.

Set a Purpose
Have students discuss the Witness History Selection. Point out the Section Focus Question, and have students fill in the Note Taking graphic organizer.

Preview Key Terms
Preview the section's Key Terms.

Instructional Resources
❑ **WITNESS HISTORY** Audio CD

❑ **All in One Teaching Resources**
   L3 Preread the Chapter, p. 9
   L3 Analyze Visuals, p. 11
   L3 Vocabulary Builder, p. 12

❑ **Reading and Note Taking Study Guide**
(On-Level, Adapted, and Spanish)
Section 1

TEACH

Axis and Allies Plan Strategy
Understand the "Europe First" strategy.

Turning the Tide in Europe
Discuss Allied victories in the Atlantic.

Increasing the Pressure on Germany
Explain the advances and difficulties the Allies faced while fighting in Italy and Germany.

Turning the Tide in the Pacific
Describe the effects of the Battle of Midway.

Instructional Resources
❑ **All in One Teaching Resources**
   L3 Geography and History: North Africa, p. 16
❑ **Skills Handbook**
   L3 Synthesize Information, p. 31
❑ **Color Transparencies**
   L3 The Battle of Midway
❑ **Note Taking Transparencies,** B-114

ASSESS/RETEACH

Assess Progress
Evaluate student comprehension with the Section Assessment and Section Quiz.

Reteach
Assign the Reading and Note Taking Study Guide to help struggling students.

Extend
Have students research one of the major Allied victories and present their findings in reports.

Instructional Resources
❑ **All in One Teaching Resources**
   L3 Section Quiz, p. 23
❑ **Reading and Note Taking Study Guide**
(On-Level, Adapted, and Spanish)
Section 1 Summary
❑ **Progress Monitoring Transparencies,** 110

WORLD WAR II 1941–1945

2. The Home Front

Pacing
1.5 periods
.75 block

| L1 Special Needs |
| L2 Basic to Average |
| L3 All Students |
| L4 Average to Advanced |

Section Objectives

- Explain how World War II increased opportunities for women and minorities.

- Analyze the effects of the war on civil liberties for Japanese Americans and others.

- Examine how the need to support the war effort changed American lives.

Terms and People • A. Philip Randolph • Executive Order 8802 • bracero program • internment • *Korematsu* v. *United States* • 442nd Regimental Combat Team • rationing • OWI

Focus Question: How did the war change America at home?

PREPARE TO READ

Build Background Knowledge
Preview the section and remind students that World War II, more than the New Deal, brought the United States out of the Great Depression.

Set a Purpose
Have students discuss the Witness History Selection. Point out the Section Focus Question, and have students fill in the Note Taking graphic organizer.

Preview Key Terms
Preview the section's Key Terms.

Instructional Resources
❑ **WITNESS HISTORY** Audio CD

❑ **All in One Teaching Resources**
❑ **Reading and Note Taking Study Guide**
(On-Level, Adapted, and Spanish)
Section 2

TEACH

New Economic Opportunities
Discuss how the war effort in the United States changed the lives of women and minorities.

Workers on the Move
Describe regional population shifts.

A Challenge to Civil Liberties
Explore the discrimination that German, Italian, and Japanese immigrants faced.

Supporting the War Effort
Describe government control of the economy.

Instructional Resources

❑ **All in One Teaching Resources**
L3 Biography: Navajo Code Talkers, p. 17
L3 Landmark Decisions of the Supreme Court: Can government limit a group's liberties during wartime?, p. 18
❑ **Color Transparencies**
L3 Victory Gardens
❑ **Note Taking Transparencies,** B-115

ASSESS/RETEACH

Assess Progress
Evaluate student comprehension with the Section Assessment and Section Quiz.

Reteach
Assign the Reading and Note Taking Study Guide to help struggling students.

Extend
Have students complete the Enrichment worksheet and compare the experiences of children during the war.

Instructional Resources

❑ **All in One Teaching Resources**
L4 Enrichment: Role of Children, p. 14
L3 Section Quiz, p. 24
❑ **Reading and Note Taking Study Guide**
(On-Level, Adapted, and Spanish)
Section 2 Summary
❑ **Progress Monitoring Transparencies,** 111

WORLD WAR II 1941–1945

3. Victory in Europe and the Pacific

Pacing
2.5 periods
1.25 blocks

L1	Special Needs
L2	Basic to Average
L3	All Students
L4	Average to Advanced

Section Objectives

■ Analyze the planning and impact of the D-Day invasion of France.

■ Understand how the Allies achieved final victory in Europe.

■ Explore the reasons President Truman decided to use the atomic bomb against Japan.

Terms and People • D-Day • Battle of the Bulge • Harry S. Truman • island hopping • kamikaze • Albert Einstein • Manhattan Project • J. Robert Oppenheimer

Focus Question: How did the Allies defeat the Axis Powers?

PREPARE TO READ

Build Background Knowledge
Preview the section, and remind students that while the Germans were on the defensive in Europe, Japanese forces controlled many Pacific islands.

Set a Purpose
Have students discuss the Witness History Selection. Point out the Section Focus Question, and have students fill in the Note Taking graphic organizer.

Preview Key Terms
Preview the section's Key Terms.

Instructional Resources
❏ **WITNESS HISTORY** Audio CD
❏ **All in One Teaching Resources**
   L3 Reading Strategy, p. 13
❏ **Reading and Note Taking Study Guide**
   (On-Level, Adapted, and Spanish)
   Section 3

TEACH

Planning Germany's Defeat
Describe how FDR, Stalin, and Churchill reached an agreement to fight Germany.

D-Day Invasion of Normandy
Discuss the effects of the D-Day invasion.

Liberation of Europe
Explain how the Allies defeated Germany.

Advancing in the Pacific
Describe the U.S. island-hopping strategy.

The Atomic Bomb Ends the War
Discuss various reactions to the use of atomic weapons, and the bombs' effects.

Instructional Resources
❏ **All in One Teaching Resources**
   L1 L2 Biography: Ira Hayes, p. 19
   L3 Biography: The Marines at Iwo Jima, p. 20
❏ **Color Transparencies**
   The Manhattan Project
   The Allies Win the War
❏ **Note Taking Transparencies,** B-116

ASSESS/RETEACH

Assess Progress
Evaluate student comprehension with the Section Assessment and Section Quiz.

Reteach
Assign the Reading and Note Taking Study Guide to help struggling students.

Extend
Extend the lesson by having students complete the online activity on using atomic weapons.

Instructional Resources
❏ **All in One Teaching Resources**
   L3 Section Quiz, p. 25
❏ **Reading and Note Taking Study Guide**
   (On-Level, Adapted, and Spanish)
   Section 3 Summary
❏ **Progress Monitoring Transparencies,** 112

Name _____ Class _____ Date _____ M T W T F

WORLD WAR II 1941–1945

4. The Holocaust

Pacing
2 periods
1 block

| L1 Special Needs |
| L2 Basic to Average |
| L3 All Students |
| L4 Average to Advanced |

Section Objectives

- Trace the roots and progress of Hitler's campaign against the Jews.
- Explore the goals of Hitler's "final solution" and the nature of the Nazi death camps.
- Examine how the United States responded to the Holocaust.

Terms and People • Holocaust • Nuremberg Laws • Kristallnacht • genocide • concentration camp • death camp • War Refugee Board

Focus Question: How did the Holocaust develop and what were its results?

PREPARE TO READ

Build Background Knowledge
Preview the section, and remind students that treaties ending World War I caused economic and political upheavals in Germany.

Set a Purpose
Have students discuss the Witness History Selection. Point out the Section Focus Question, and have students fill in the Note Taking graphic organizer.

Preview Key Terms
Preview the section's Key Terms.

Instructional Resources
❏ **WITNESS HISTORY** Audio CD
❏ **All in One Teaching Resources**
❏ **Reading and Note Taking Study Guide**
(On-Level, Adapted, and Spanish)
Section 4

TEACH

Roots of the Holocaust
Explain Hitler's persecution of Jews in Germany.

Nazis Adopt the "Final Solution"
Discuss the Nazis' systematic plan to eliminate the Jews.

The Allies and the Holocaust
Describe how Allied reactions to the Holocaust changed throughout the war.

Instructional Resources
❏ **All in One Teaching Resources**
   L3 Link to Literature: *Night*, p. 21
❏ **Note Taking Transparencies,** B-117a, B117b

ASSESS/RETEACH

Assess Progress
Evaluate student comprehension with the Section Assessment and Section Quiz.

Reteach
Assign the Reading and Note Taking Study Guide to help struggling students.

Extend
Have students present an oral report on a nonfiction book about the Holocaust.

Instructional Resources
❏ **All in One Teaching Resources**
   L3 Section Quiz, p. 26
❏ **Reading and Note Taking Study Guide**
(On-Level, Adapted, and Spanish)
Section 4 Summary
❏ **Progress Monitoring Transparencies,** 113

WORLD WAR II 1941–1945

5. Effects of the War

Pacing
2 periods
1 block

L1	Special Needs
L2	Basic to Average
L3	All Students
L4	Average to Advanced

Section Objectives

■ Trace the roots and progress of Hitler's campaign against the Jews.

■ Explore the goals of Hitler's "final solution" and the nature of the Nazi death camps.

■ Examine how the United States responded to the Holocaust.

Terms and People • Yalta Conference • superpower • GATT • UN • Universal Declaration of Human Rights • Geneva Convention • Nuremberg Trials

Focus Question: What were the major immediate and long-term effects of World War II?

PREPARE TO READ

Build Background Knowledge
Preview the section, and remind students that before t World War II, many Americans favored isolationism.

Set a Purpose
Have students discuss the Witness History Selection. Point out the Section Focus Question, and have students fill in the Note Taking graphic organizer.

Preview Key Terms
Preview the section's Key Terms.

Instructional Resources
❑ **WITNESS HISTORY** Audio CD

❑ **All in One Teaching Resources**
❑ **Reading and Note Taking Study Guide**
(On-Level, Adapted, and Spanish)
Section 5

TEACH

Allies Set Postwar Goals
Explain decisions made at Yalta and Potsdam.

A New World Takes Shape
Discuss the rise of the United States and the Soviet Union as world superpowers.

International Cooperation
Describe the formation of the United Nations and the trials of Axis leaders and soldiers.

A New American Identity
Discuss how World War II gave Americans a broader world view.

Instructional Resources
❑ **All in One Teaching Resources**
　L3 History Comics: Postwar Goals, p. 22
❑ **Color Transparencies**
　L3 Dividing Germany
❑ **Note Taking Transparencies,** B-118

ASSESS/RETEACH

Assess Progress
Evaluate student comprehension with the Section Assessment and Section Quiz.

Reteach
Assign the Reading and Note Taking Study Guide to help struggling students.

Extend
Have students write a short essay about the achievements in the last five years of a UN-sponsored program.

Instructional Resources
❑ **All in One Teaching Resources**
　L3 Section Quiz, p. 27
　L1 L2 Chapter Test A, p. 28
　L3 Chapter Test B, p. 31
❑ **Reading and Note Taking Study Guide**
(On-Level, Adapted, and Spanish)
Section 5 Summary
❑ **Progress Monitoring Transparencies,** 114

WORLD WAR II

Preread the Chapter: Why and How?

What is **Prereading?** It is a reading comprehension strategy. This graphic organizer aids you in prereading this chapter.

Checklist: *Place a check on the line when you have completed the following:*

_____ Read all items in the Chapter Opener.

_____ Read the titles of the charts, graphs, maps, and timeline in the Quick Study Guide and Concept Connector Cumulative Review.

_____ Read the chapter assessment.

Before you read each section of your text, look at the following material. (Chapters may have 3, 4, or 5 sections.) Check the sections as you complete the review.

Sections: 1_____ 2_____ 3_____ 4_____ 5_____ Read the Focus Question, the section opener information in the side column, and each boldface heading and subheading.

Sections: 1_____ 2_____ 3_____ 4_____ 5_____ Looked over all words that are underlined or in boldface type.

Sections: 1_____ 2_____ 3_____ 4_____ 5_____ Read all review questions within the section.

Complete the following:

1. Chapter title: _____

2. Write the main idea of each section based on its Focus Question.

Section 1: _____

_____

Section 2: _____

_____

Section 3: _____

_____

Section 4: _____

_____

Section 5: _____

_____

Name _____ Class _____ Date _____

Preread the Chapter: Why and How? *(Continued)*

3. List three visual aids included in the chapter (e.g., pictures, maps, charts, diagrams, features). Describe how they will aid your understanding of the chapter.

(1) _____

_____

(2) _____

_____

(3) _____

_____

4. Describe one new or important idea you learned from reading the Quick Study Guide.

_____

_____

5. Identify two unfamiliar words that you noticed during your prereading, and determine from the context what you think the new word means.

Word #1 _____ Part of Speech _____

Clues to meaning _____

Predicted meaning _____

Word #2 _____ Part of Speech _____

Clues to meaning _____

Predicted meaning _____

6. After previewing this chapter, were you able to understand what the chapter is about?

Not understood _____ Somewhat understood _____ Easily understood _____

7. Copy the heading (titles in blue print) that you predict will be the most difficult to understand.

_____

_____

8. How many pages are in the chapter? _____

9. Estimate the time it will take you to read the chapter. _____

Name _____ Class _____ Date _____

Analyze Visuals

Images are an effective way to communicate information. There are many types of visuals, such as photographs, paintings, and Infographics. Visuals tell a story in a dramatic or vivid style. Just as with any primary or secondary source, it is important to look closely and ask questions to determine the meaning and reliability of the visual.

Use this outline to help you better understand ideas or events conveyed by a visual. Answer these questions to the best of your ability.

Title of visual Page

1. What is the topic of the visual (what is happening)?

   _____

2. Focus on the details and list three that you find in the visual. How does each help convey information about the topic?

   _____

   _____

   _____

3. Assume you are one of the individuals in the picture, or that you were present when the image was made.

   (a) Describe who you are.

   _____

   (b) Explain what your reaction might have been to the situation.

   _____

   _____

4. The creator often reveals a bias about the subject or an attempt to get a response from the viewer. Is there anything you see in the image that tells the creator's point of view?

   _____

   _____

5. Write your own caption for the image.

   _____

Name _____ Class _____ Date _____

Analyze Visuals

Images are an effective way to communicate information. There are many types of visuals, such as photographs, paintings, and Infographics. Visuals tell a story in a dramatic or vivid style. Just as with any primary or secondary source, it is important to look closely and ask questions to determine the meaning and reliability of the visual.

Use this outline to help you better understand ideas or events conveyed by a visual. Answer these questions to the best of your ability.

Title of visual Page

1. What is the topic of the visual (what is happening)?

   _____

2. Focus on the details and list three that you find in the visual. How does each help convey information about the topic?

   _____

   _____

   _____

3. Assume you are one of the individuals in the picture, or that you were present when the image was made.

   (a) Describe who you are.

   _____

   (b) Explain what your reaction might have been to the situation.

   _____

   _____

4. The creator often reveals a bias about the subject or an attempt to get a response from the viewer. Is there anything you see in the image that tells the creator's point of view?

   _____

   _____

5. Write your own caption for the image.

   _____

Vocabulary Builder

Use Context Clues to Determine Meaning

As you read, **context clues** can help you figure out the meaning of unfamiliar words. Context clues are words and phrases in the surrounding text that clarify the meaning of other words. Using context clues allows you to get the main idea of new vocabulary while you continue reading. Then you can go back and use a dictionary to check the meaning of unfamiliar words.

The example below shows how the word *simultaneously* is used in your text, identifies context clues, and provides a possible meaning.

> **Example**
> Patton's forces advanced east with heightened confidence. <u>Simultaneously</u>, the British pressed westward from Egypt, trapping Axis forces in a continually shrinking pocket in Tunisia. Rommel escaped, but his army did not.
> **Context clues** Patton's forces advanced east; the British pressed westward
> **What the clues tell me** These things happened at the same time.
> **Possible meaning** at the same time

Directions: *Review the words listed below in your text. Identify context clues from the text for each word, and record those clues in the table. Then, write a possible meaning for each word.*

Word	Clues	Possible Meaning
1. momentum		
2. prevail		
3. comprise		
4. scenario		
5. priority		
6. restraint		
7. undergo		
8. predominant		

WORLD WAR II
Reading Stategy

Recognize Sequence

In the study of history, it is important to develop an understanding of the sequence in which important events took place. Identifying sequences of related events will help you comprehend the relationships between these events and understand how they may have influenced one another.

History textbooks often arrange information in chronological order, or the order in which the events took place. Signal words such as *first, before,* and *later* can provide clues about the sequence of events discussed in a passage. One way to clarify a sequence of events is to organize the information in a sequence chart.

Read the following passage with some italicized signal words:

Germany attacked Russia *beginning* in 1941. The Germans sent one army north toward the city of Leningrad. A second army traveled toward Moscow, *while* a third army moved south toward Stalingrad. As the German troops moved deeper into the Soviet Union, they encountered fierce resistance fighting and harsh weather conditions. By 1942, Hitler decided to focus the campaign on southern Russia. However, German forces *once again* encountered a strong counterattack *while* attempting to capture Stalingrad, and were forced to surrender in February of 1943.

A sequence chart of the events described in the paragraph might look like this:

Germany attacks Russia in 1941, sending three armies toward Russian cities.

↓

After facing harsh conditions and fierce resistance, Hitler decides to focus campaign on southern Russia in 1942.

↓

Ferocious struggle for Stalingrad forces German troops to surrender in February 1943.

Directions: *Read the paragraphs in Section 3 under the subheading "Allies Push to Victory." On a separate sheet of paper, create a chart showing the sequence of events described in the passage. Then, answer the questions that follow.*

Hint: Remember to look for sequence words as you read.

1. What event took place in January 1945?

_____

_____

2. What signal word indicates that the Allies advanced north in Italy in January?

_____

3. How long after Mussolini tried to flee to Switzerland was the V-E day celebration?

_____

Enrichment: Role of Children

Children During World War II

During World War II, as government officials planned military campaigns and soldiers fought in battles around the world, children in the both the United States and Nazi Germany represented an important part of their nations' war efforts. Despite the vastly different goals of the two countries and their respective leaders, both sides recognized the significance of young people to the continued success of their ideals.

In Nazi Germany, the experiences of children varied significantly, depending on their race, ethnicity, and religion. Hitler hoped to educate children of Aryan descent in his Nazi ideology. In doing so, he hoped to develop a large group of young people devoted to the goals of the state. Jewish children, or others that the Nazis deemed "unfit," could be sent into slavery or even to Nazi death camps.

Children in the United States were educated in the importance of patriotism and democracy. The U.S. government also encouraged young people to participate in activities to bolster the war effort, such as planting victory gardens and collecting scrap metal for recycling.

Your assignment: Work alone or with partners to research the lives of children living in the United States and Nazi Germany during World War II. Use your findings to write diary entries from the perspective of both an American and a German child during World War II.

Suggested materials: Use the chart on the next page to guide your research and record your findings about the lives of children in the United States and Nazi Germany during World War II. When you have completed your research, write your diary entries on a separate sheet of paper.

Suggested procedures: You may want to consider answering some of the following questions in your entries:

- How has the outbreak of World War II changed life for my family and me?
- What have my experiences taught me about the war and the reasons it is taking place?
- What are my predictions for the outcome of the war?
- How might the war be affecting life for people in other parts of the world?

When your diary entries are complete, present them to the class. Hold a class discussion in which you consider the effects of World War II on children in both the United States and Nazi Germany.

WORLD WAR II

Enrichment: Role of Children

Children During World War II

Children in World War II			
	Children in the United States	Children in Nazi Germany	Source of Information
		Jewish	Others	
Education				
Activities				
Expectations				
Perspective on World War II				

Geography and History

The geography of North Africa presented unique challenges to the officers and troops that served there during World War II. The mountainous terrain and large deserts of the region proved very different than the more familiar conditions of warfare in Europe. Commanders such as German general Erwin Rommel and American general George S. Patton, Jr., became known for their abilities to guide troops through these challenging environments. ◆ *Use the map below and the Focus on Geography map in Section 1 of your book to answer the questions that follow on a separate sheet of paper.*

North Africa

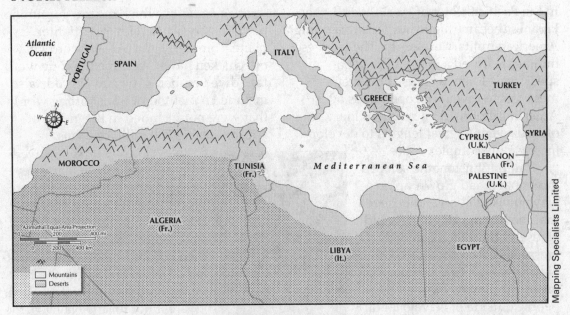

Questions to Think About

1. What landforms made fighting in Africa a different challenge for the American armed forces than fighting in Europe?

2. What landforms would Allied forces in the 1942 offensive from Casablanca, Morocco to Tunisia have had to cross?

3. **Draw Conclusions** Why might Allied leaders in North Africa have kept the paths of their offensives close to the northern tip of Africa?

WORLD WAR II
Biography

Many different groups of people came together in the United States to aid the Allied war effort during World War II. One such group was a corps of about 400 Navajos who served as radio operators and transmitted messages in code, using the Navajo language and a series of other terms that they created themselves. ♦ *As you read, think about how the Navajo code talkers contributed to the Allied war effort. Then, on a separate sheet of paper, answer the questions that follow.*

Navajo Code Talkers

In the Pacific theater of World War II, the Japanese became highly skilled at decoding American military messages. The Japanese military featured a group of English-speaking soldiers who used intercepted messages to thwart the operations of American troops. As a result, military officials went to great lengths to develop increasingly complex codes.

Philip Johnston, the son of a missionary, had grown up on a Navajo reservation and believed that the Navajo language could be useful for relaying coded messages for two reasons. One, Navajo was an oral language of great complexity. Two, very few people outside of Navajo lands could understand it. Johnston took his idea to the Marines in 1942, and the Marines agreed to begin recruiting Navajo men as radio operators and code talkers.

The first group of code talkers included 29 Navajo Marines. The code included about 200 terms, most of which were common Navajo words that were given new meanings related to military operations. For instance, the code used the Navajo

Navajo code talkers, © CORBIS

term *da-he-tih-hi*, which meant "humming-bird" in Navajo, to refer to a "fighter plane." Similarly, the Navajo word *gini*, or "chicken hawk" became the code word for "dive bomber." The Navajo code also included a method of transmitting words that were not included in the group of approximately 200 military terms.

Navajo code talkers played an important role in many key battles in the Pacific during World War II. During the first two days of battle at Iwo Jima, code talkers transmitted more than 800 messages without making an error. Following the battle, one military official recalled, "Were it not for the Navajos, the Marines would never have taken Iwo Jima."

Despite their important contributions, the Navajo code talkers went largely unrecognized for many years. Because the code was so valuable to the military, it remained a classified secret until 1968. In recent years, government leaders have begun to officially recognize the significance of the code talkers to the Allied victory in World War II.

Questions to Think About

1. How did the code talkers develop the original version of the Navajo code?

2. Why were the contributions of the Navajo code talkers unrecognized for many years following the war?

3. Explain Problems Why would Japanese code breakers have had difficulty deciphering the Navajo code?

Landmark Decisions of the Supreme Court: Can Government Limit a Group's Liberties During Wartime?

Korematsu v. *United States*

In the case of *Korematsu* v. *United States*, the Supreme Court had to decide whether the need for wartime security justified the internment of people of Japanese ancestry. Fred Korematsu, a young American citizen of Japanese ancestry, had refused to report for relocation on the grounds of his U.S. citizenship. He was eventually arrested and held in a relocation camp while his case went to the Supreme Court. The Supreme Court ultimately split 6–3 to uphold the government's right to force internment of a particular racial or cultural group for security purposes. ◆ *Read the following excerpts from Supreme Court justices who decided the case. On a separate sheet of paper, answer the questions at the bottom of this page.*

To cast this case into outlines of racial prejudice, without reference to the real military dangers which were presented, merely confuses the issue. Korematsu was not excluded from the Military Area because of hostility to him or his race. He was excluded because we are at war with the Japanese Empire, because the properly constituted military authorities feared an invasion of our West Coast and felt constrained to take proper security measures, because they decided that the military urgency of the situation demanded that all citizens of Japanese ancestry be segregated from the West Coast temporarily, and finally, because Congress, reposing its confidence in this time of war in our military leaders—as inevitably it must—determined that they should have the power to do just this.

—*Justice Hugo Black*

Individuals must not be left impoverished of their constitutional rights on a plea of military necessity that has neither substance nor support. . . . Civilian Exclusion Order No. 34, banishing from a prescribed area of the Pacific Coast "all persons of Japanese ancestry, both alien and non-alien," . . . Being an obvious racial discrimination, . . . deprives all those within its scope of the equal protection of the laws as guaranteed by the Fifth Amendment. . . . I dissent, therefore, from this legalization of racism. . . . All residents of this nation are kin in some way by blood or culture to a foreign land. Yet they are primarily and necessarily a part of the new and distinct civilization of the United States. They must accordingly be treated at all times as the heirs of the American experiment and as entitled to all the rights and freedoms guaranteed by the Constitution.

—*Justice Frank Murphy*

Questions to Think About

1. On what does Judge Black argue that the internment order is based?

2. Why does Judge Murphy disagree with the decision of the court?

3. Activity Write an editorial responding to the *Korematsu* v. *United States* decision. You should either support or oppose the decision and use the opinions of the Supreme Court justices to support your arguments.

WORLD WAR II
Biography

In February and March 1945, United States Marines took part in one of the fiercest battles of the war's Pacific campaign. On the small island of Iwo Jima, marines battled with Japanese forces for 36 days. Only about 650 miles from Japan's capital of Tokyo, the Japanese forces were determined to not lose ground. Despite more than 23,000 marine casualties, American forces won. A photograph of six soldiers raising an American flag on the island remains a symbol of the American victory and the troops who gave their lives for it. One of the soldiers pictured was Ira Hayes, a young Pima Indian marine.

◆ *As you read, think about how Ira Hayes' life changed during his service in World War II. Then, on a separate sheet of paper, answer the questions that follow.*

Ira Hayes (1923–1955)

A full blood Pima Indian, Ira Hayes was born on the Pima Reservation in Sacaton, Arizona, on January 12, 1923. He had rarely left the boundaries of the reservation at the time he enlisted in the United States Marines in 1942. After joining the marines, Hayes trained to be a paratrooper, and in 1943 he was sent to the Pacific.

Ira Hayes, © Bettmann/CORBIS

Hayes became well known for his role in the battle on the island of Iwo Jima. It was here that Hayes took part in the flag raising captured in a famous photograph of the battle. Joseph Rosenthal, a photographer covering the war for the Associated Press, took the picture on February 23, 1945. Hayes and his fellow soldiers planted the flag on top of Mount Suribachi, where it could be seen from all around the island.

Eventually, Rosenthal's photograph became a defining image of the battle, and Ira Hayes became a hero of World War II. As a result of his role in raising the flag, President Roosevelt asked Hayes and the other surviving soldiers in the photograph to return to the United States to participate in a war bond drive.

Hayes remained humble even though he was often praised for his heroic role in such an important event. He pointed out that his role in this event did not make him feel heroic or proud: "How could I feel like a hero when only five men in my platoon of 45 survived, when only 27 men in my company of 250 managed to escape death or injury?" Hayes even went so far as to suggest, "sometimes I wish that guy had never made that picture."

Questions to Think About

1. What was Hayes' life like before he joined the Marines?

2. Where did Hayes and his fellow soldiers raise the American flag on Iwo Jima?

3. Detect Points of View Why do you think Hayes said he did not feel like a hero? Why might he have said that he wished the photograph had never been taken?

WORLD WAR II

Biography

As their strategy of island hopping brought Allied troops closer to the Japanese mainland, the small island of Iwo Jima was to become a valuable stronghold from which aircraft could take off and make emergency landings. Winning the island was a bitter struggle.
◆ *As you read, think about the sacrifices made by the marines who fought at Iwo Jima. Then, on a separate sheet of paper, answer the questions that follow.*

The Marines at Iwo Jima

As approximately 70,000 United States troops prepared for an invasion of the Japanese-controlled island of Iwo Jima, a force of more than 20,000 Japanese soldiers had entrenched themselves in the island's mountains and built tunnels throughout the island. As a result, when the first U.S. troops began to land on Iwo Jima on February 19, 1945, they encountered strong resistance from the Japanese. Defending themselves against enemy fire proved difficult as they stormed the island from the sea.

Iwo Jima flag raising, © CORBIS

However, in the coming days marines began to make progress in their efforts to win the island. By February 23, they had captured Mount Suribachi, a tall volcanic mountain that provided a strategic defensive location for Japanese troops. Photographer Joseph Rosenthal took the famous picture of six American soldiers raising the United States flag at the top of Mount Suribachi. This photograph has come to represent the heroism of the soldiers who fought at Iwo Jima. After more than a month of fighting, the United States won the battle for the island.

The victory came at a significant cost. Approximately 6,000 were killed in the battle, while more than 20,000 were injured. The battle for Iwo Jima became one of the most costly battles of the war for the United States. About one-third of all marines that lost their lives during World War II did so at Iwo Jima. Such significant loss of American lives at Iwo Jima and in other similar battles in the Pacific contributed to the later decision to use the atomic bomb rather than launch an invasion of mainland Japan.

Despite the costliness of the fighting at Iwo Jima, the victory did prove to be a significant one for American forces. The subsequent use of the island for carrying out air attacks against Japan, as well as for landing damaged planes returning from such attacks, proved especially valuable. The victory also provided a rallying point for the American public. Chester Nimitz, commander of the United States Navy in the Pacific said of the soldiers, "Among the men who fought on Iwo Jima, uncommon valor was a common virtue."

Questions to Think About

1. Why was it difficult for American forces to defend themselves against Japanese fire?

2. What event did Joseph Rosenthal capture in his famous photograph?

3. **Summarize** Why was Iwo Jima an important strategic location for the United States campaign in the Pacific?

WORLD WAR II
Link to Literature

Elie Wiesel was born in Romania in 1928 and grew up in the town of Sighet. When he was a teenager, Wiesel and his family were sent to concentration camps during the Holocaust. Members of his family were killed at Auschwitz and Buchenwald. Wiesel was still being held at Buchenwald when the camp was liberated in April 1945. He later became a United States citizen in 1963 and eventually became a college professor. Wiesel has published a number of works that discuss the Holocaust. The excerpt below comes from Wiesel's autobiographical work *Night*. In it, Wiesel describes his daily life at Auschwitz. ◆ *As you read, think about how the conditions Wiesel describes would affect the people facing them over a long period of time. Then, on a separate sheet of paper, answer the questions that follow.*

Night

We had just returned from work. As soon as we passed the camp's entrance, we sensed something out of the ordinary in the air. The roll call was shorter than usual. The evening soup was distributed with great speed, swallowed as quickly.

I was no longer in the same block as my father. They had transferred me to another Kommando, the construction one, where, twelve hours a day I hauled heavy slabs of stone. The head of my new block was a German Jew, small with piercing eyes. That evening he announced to us that henceforth no one was allowed to leave the block after the evening soup. A terrible word began to circulate thereafter: selection.

We knew what that meant. An SS would examine us. Whenever he found someone extremely frail—a "Muselman" was what we called those inmates—he would write down his number: good for the crematorium.

After the soup, we gathered between the bunks. The veterans told us:

"You're lucky to have been brought here so late. Today this is paradise compared to what the camp was like two years ago. Back then, Buna was a veritable hell. No water, no blankets, less soup and bread. At night, we slept almost naked and the temperature was thirty below. We were collecting corpses by the hundreds every day. Work was very hard. Today, this is a little paradise. The Kapos back then had orders to kill a certain number of prisoners each day. And every week, selection. A merciless selection. . . . Yes, you are lucky."

"Enough! Be quiet!" I begged them. "Tell your stories tomorrow, or some other day."

They burst out laughing. They were not veterans for nothing.

"Are you scared? We too were scared. And, at that time, for good reason."

The old men stayed in their corner, silent, motionless, hunted-down creatures. Some were praying.

One more hour. Then we would know the verdict: death or reprieve.

And my father? I first thought of him now. How would he pass the selection? He had aged so much . . .

Source: Excerpt from NIGHT by Elie Wiesel, translated by Marion Wiesel.

Questions to Think About

1. What does Wiesel do every day in the camp?

2. Which facts cause Wiesel to express concern about his father's safety?

3. Draw Conclusions What does Wiesel imply about the veterans' ability to survive?

WORLD WAR II

History Comics

As fighting wound down, the leaders of Russia, the United States, and Great Britain came together to discuss strategy for the end of the war and begin planning for life in the postwar era in Germany and Eastern Europe. ◆ *Use the information in the paragraph and your knowledge of history to write captions for each comic panel about the meetings at Yalta and Potsdam.*

Postwar Goals

MAKING DECISIONS FOR THE POSTWAR WORLD

Postwar Goals, Chris Vallo

_____   _____   _____

_____   _____   _____

_____   _____   _____

_____   _____   _____

Critical Thinking

In the space below, explain how people in Poland and Germany might have felt about the decisions made at the conferences.

WORLD WAR II

Section 1 Quiz

A. Key Terms and People

Directions: *Match the descriptions in Column I with the terms in Column II. Write the letter of the correct answer in the blank provided.*

Column I

_____ 1. dropping large amounts of bombs to inflict maximum damage

_____ 2. general known as Blood and Guts

_____ 3. dropping bombs that target key political and industrial centers

_____ 4. accepting defeat without any concessions

_____ 5. led the Allied invasion of North Africa

_____ 6. U.S. naval commander

Column II

a. Dwight Eisenhower

b. George S. Patton, Jr.

c. unconditional surrender

d. saturation bombing

e. strategic bombing

f. Chester Nimitz

B. Key Concepts

Directions: *Write the letter of the correct answer or ending in the blank provided.*

_____ 7. The Allies decided to pursue a "Europe First" strategy because they
   a. thought that Germany was closer to surrendering than Japan was.
   b. believed that Germany posed a more serious threat than Japan did.
   c. knew that it would be easier to ship supplies to Europe than to the Pacific.
   d. understood that fighting a two-front war was impossible.

_____ 8. Following the battle of Stalingrad,
   a. German troops continued their blitzkrieg eastward.
   b. Hitler controlled the Caucasus oil fields.
   c. both German and Soviet troops refused to surrender.
   d. Hitler's plans of dominating Europe were ended.

_____ 9. Allied bombing of Germany in 1942 changed the war because it
   a. helped pave the way for a later all-out offensive.
   b. allowed the Allies to avoid fighting in Italy.
   c. permitted German forces to occupy the best defensive positions.
   d. placed additional pressure on Soviet troops.

_____ 10. Which of the following was a result of the Battle of Midway?
   a. Japan gained a powerful navy and fortified positions.
   b. The United States lost many aircraft carriers and aircraft.
   c. The United States was put on the defensive end of the war.
   d. Japan never again threatened Pacific domination.

Name _____ Class _____ Date _____

Section 2 Quiz

A. Key Terms and People

Directions: *Choose the term or person that best matches the underlined phrase. You will not use all of the answers.*

Column I

_____ 1. limiting the amount of certain goods that civilians can buy

_____ 2. ensured fair hiring practices in jobs funded with government money

_____ 3. worked with the media to encourage support for the war effort

_____ 4. policy of temporary imprisoning members of a specific group

_____ 5. plan to bring laborers from Mexico to work on American farms

_____ 6. African American labor leader

Column II

a. A. Philip Randolph

b. Executive Order 8802

c. bracero program

d. internment

e. *Korematsu* v. *United States*

f. 442nd Regimental Combat Team

g. rationing

h. OWI

B. Key Concepts

Directions: *Write the letter of the correct answer or ending in the blank provided.*

_____ 7. How did wartime pressures create a break from the past?

    a. All women quit their jobs once they married to raise large families.

    b. Many women took nontraditional jobs.

    c. Women had to give up their jobs to returning soldiers.

    d. Most children stayed in day-care centers.

_____ 8. During World War II, many African Americans

    a. found work with national defense employers.

    b. carried out a large protest march on Washington, D.C.

    c. left organizations dedicated to promoting equal rights.

    d. joined organizations dedicated to fighting segregation.

_____ 9. Executive Order 9066 affected civil liberties in the United States because it

    a. forced hundreds of Italian Americans into camps.

    b. removed Germans and Italians from the enemy aliens list.

    c. designated war zones from which anyone could be removed.

    d. allowed Japanese Americans to enlist in the armed forces.

_____ 10. Who created the Office of Price Administration?

    a. Ted Nakashima   c. Franklin Roosevelt

    b. A. Philip Randolph   d. Gov. Earl Warren

WORLD WAR II

Section 3 Quiz

A. Key Terms and People

Directions: *Use the terms and people in the word bank to complete the sentences below. You will not use all of the answers.*

D-Day	island hopping	Manhattan Project
Battle of the Bulge	kamikaze	J. Robert Oppenheimer
Harry S. Truman	Albert Einstein	

1. _____ became President after FDR's death.

2. The _____ was the program to develop an atomic bomb.

3. _____ signed a letter to President Roosevelt, explaining the importance of atomic development.

4. On _____, the Allies launched their invasion of Normandy.

5. American forces in the Pacific followed an _____ strategy.

6. _____ was an attempt to drive a wedge between American and British forces.

B. Key Concepts

Directions: *Write the letter of the correct answer or ending in the blank provided.*

_____ 7. What was one effect of the D-Day invasion?

    a. Japan knew that Germany was out of the war.

    b. Germany could never again attack the Allies.

    c. The Allies took an important step toward reaching Berlin.

    d. Soviet troops stopped pushing toward Germany from the West.

_____ 8. One of the effects of the Battle of the Bulge was that

    a. Germany used its reserves and demoralized its troops in the battle.

    b. British and American troops had little difficulty approaching Berlin.

    c. Germany prolonged the time before its surrender to the Allies.

    d. Soviet troops avoided the Oder River outside Berlin.

_____ 9. As American forces approached Japan, the Japanese forces

    a. won an important victory in the Philippines.

    b. conquered every island the United States held.

    c. surrendered quickly and joined the Allied forces.

    d. fought almost to the last, preferring killing themselves to surrender.

_____ 10. Who made the decision to use the atomic bomb against Japan?

    a. Franklin D. Roosevelt   **c.** Leslie Groves

    b. Harry S. Truman   **d.** Enrico Fermi

WORLD WAR II
Section 4 Quiz

A. Key Terms

Directions: *Write a definition for each of the terms listed below.*

1. Holocaust _____

2. Nuremberg Laws _____

3. Kristallnacht _____

4. genocide _____

5. concentration camp _____

6. War Refugee Board _____

B. Key Concepts

Directions: *Write the letter of the correct answer or ending in the blank provided.*

_____ 7. Hitler's economic persecution of Jews in Germany involved
   a. putting Jews into death camps.
   b. barring Jews from working in civil service.
   c. teaching "racial science" courses in schools.
   d. prohibiting marriage between Jews and non-Jews.

_____ 8. Many Jews were prevented from leaving Germany because
   a. U.S. officials denied them the right to leave the country.
   b. transportation to other countries was too expensive.
   c. some countries refused to accept them during the Great Depression.
   d. they needed to stay to protect their businesses and families.

_____ 9. What did Nazi camp administrators do to identify people from different groups in the concentration camps?
   a. Each group was sent to a different camp than other groups.
   b. Each group was assigned and wore different colored insignia.
   c. Some people had numbers tatooed onto their arms and others did not.
   d. Some groups wore vertical stripes and other groups wore horizontal stripes.

_____ 10. Which of the following limited the initial U.S. response to the Holocaust?
   a. reports of concentration camps in newspapers
   b. Roosevelt's establishment of the War Refugee Board
   c. the nation's relaxed immigration policy
   d. many people undrestimated Hitler's plans

WORLD WAR II

Section 5 Quiz

A. Key Terms

Directions: *Choose the term that best completes each sentence. You will not use all of the answers.*

Column I

_____ 1. drafted under the guidance of Eleanor Roosevelt

_____ 2. governs the treatment of wounded soldiers and prisoners of war

_____ 3. dominant countries after World War II

_____ 4. designed to expand world trade by reducing tariffs

_____ 5. legal action taken against Nazis

_____ 6. provided food and aid to much of the world

Column II

a. Yalta Conference

b. superpowers

c. GATT

d. UN

e. Universal Declaration of Human Rights

f. Geneva Convention

g. Nuremberg trials

B. Key Concepts

Directions: *Write the letter of the correct answer or ending in the blank provided.*

_____ 7. How did Japan change politically after World War II?

    a. A long-standing civil war resumed.

    b. Communist and non-communist interests clashed.

    c. Japan was divided into two different countries.

    d. A new constitution enacted democratic reforms.

_____ 8. Which two nations emerged as the strongest following World War II?

    a. Britain and France   **c.** China and Japan

    b. Soviet Union and United States   **d.** Germany and Poland

_____ 9. The United Nations was organized to

    a. punish Germany.   **c.** encourage cooperation.

    b. reprimand soldiers.   **d.** help small European nations

_____ 10. In the years closely following World War II, many African Americans

    a. called for a return to isolationism.

    b. renewed their efforts to work for civil rights.

    c. found good jobs in the booming economy.

    d. wanted the government to play a smaller role in economic affairs.

WORLD WAR II
Test A

A. Terms and People

Directions: *Match the descriptions in Column I with the terms and people in Column II. Write the letter of the correct answer in the blank provided. (3 points each)*

Column I

_____ 1. organization formed in 1945 to promote cooperation between the Great Powers

_____ 2. strategy of capturing some Japanese-held islands and ignoring others

_____ 3. limiting the amount of certain goods that civilians can buy

_____ 4. worked against African American discrimination in the United States

_____ 5. worked with the Red Cross to save many Eastern European Jews from the Holocaust

_____ 6. willful annihilation of a racial, political, or cultural group

_____ 7. African American squadron that took part in 1942 German bombing campaign

_____ 8. group of Americans of Japanese descent; most decorated military unit in U.S. history

_____ 9. meeting of the Big Three in February, 1945

_____ 10. American officer known as Ike

Column II

a. Yalta Conference

b. Tuskegee Airmen

c. A. Philip Randolph

d. rationing

e. Dwight Eisenhower

f. island hopping

g. genocide

h. War Refugee Board

i. 442nd Regimental Combat Team

j. UN

B. Key Concepts

Directions: *Write the letter of the correct answer or ending in the blank provided. (4 points each)*

_____ 11. Why did the Allies adopt a "Europe First" strategy?

    a. Only Germany was considered a serious long-term threat.

    b. Italy threatened to conquer from the eastern Adriatic to East Africa.

    c. Germany, Italy, and Japan developed a coordinated strategy for victory.

_____ 12. After the Battle of Midway, Japan

    a. no longer had a powerful navy.

    b. established a military presence in the Aleutian Islands.

    c. was on the defensive end of the war.

_____ 13. Wartime migration led to violence between Mexican American youths and off-duty sailors in

    a. Los Angeles, California.

    b. Detroit, Michigan.

    c. Poston, Arizona.

_____ 14. Which group faced the most restrictions in the United States during the war?

    a. German Americans

    b. Japanese Americans

    c. Italian Americans

_____ 15. Which leader in 1943 wanted to open a second front in Europe during the war against Germany?

    a. Franklin Roosevelt

    b. Winston Churchill

    c. Joseph Stalin

_____ 16. President Truman's military advisers predicted that an invasion of Japan

    a. could strategically target cities devoted to war production.

    b. could force the Japanese to surrender quickly.

    c. might cost as many as 1,000,000 American lives.

_____ 17. The Nuremberg Laws

    a. issued an order to attack Jewish synagogues and businesses.

    b. denied German citizenship and other rights to Jews.

    c. forced German Jews to move into ghettos.

_____ 18. In what country did General Douglas MacArthur oversee the building of a democratic government after the end of the war?

    a. Germany

    b. Italy

    c. Japan

Directions: *Use the quotation below to answer question 19.*

> "... disregard and contempt for human rights have resulted in barbarous [cruel] acts which have outraged the conscience of mankind, and the advent [beginning] of a world in which human beings shall enjoy freedom of speech and belief and freedom from fear and want has been proclaimed as the highest aspiration [aim] of the common people, ...
>
>   —*Universal Declaration of Human Rights, 1948*

_____ 19. What event may have been one of the "barbarous acts" that influenced the writing of the Universal Declaration of Human Rights?

    a. the Holocaust

    b. the D-Day Invasion

    c. the Yalta Conference

_____ **20.** Which nation became a permanent member of the United Nations
Security Council?
   a. Germany
   b. the Soviet Union
   c. India

C. Document-Based Assessment

Directions: *Use the poster below and your knowledge of social studies to answer the following
question on a separate sheet of paper. (10 points)*

Illinois Digital Archives/Illinois State Library

21. Interpret Images What does this poster encourage people to do? How does the
poster accomplish this?

D. Critical Thinking

Directions: *Answer the following questions on a separate sheet of paper. (10 points each)*

22. Contrast What was the Allies' unified strategy for winning the war? Why did
the Axis powers fail to develop a unified strategy for winning the war?

23. Summarize In what ways did the lives of American women change during World
War II? In what ways did life change for African Americans?

WORLD WAR II

Test B

A. Key Terms and People

Directions: *Match the descriptions in Column I with the terms and people in Column II. Write the letter of the correct answer in the blank provided. You will not use all of the answers. (3 points each)*

Column I

_____ 1. energetic American officer

_____ 2. strategy used for capturing strategic Pacific locations

_____ 3. campaigned against discriminatory practices in the United States

_____ 4. Big Three meeting to discuss postwar plans

_____ 5. famous African American squadron

_____ 6. limiting the amount of certain goods that civilians can buy

_____ 7. all-Nisei unit; most decorated military unit in U.S. history

_____ 8. willful annihilation of a racial, political, or cultural group

_____ 9. U.S. organization designed to aid Eastern European Jews

_____ 10. fostered cooperation between the Great Powers

Column II

a. Erwin Rommel

b. Tuskegee Airmen

c. 442nd Regimental Combat Team

d. A. Philip Randolph

e. bracero program

f. rationing

g. internment

h. War Refugee Board

i. Dwight Eisenhower

j. genocide

k. island hopping

l. UN

m. Yalta Conference

B. Key Concepts

Directions: *Write the letter of the correct answer or ending in the blank provided. (4 points each)*

_____ 11. The Allies adopted a "Europe First" strategy because

    a. Japan's victory at the Battle of Coral Sea had frustrated Allied objectives.

    b. Germany, Italy, and Japan developed a coordinated strategy for victory.

    c. Italy threatened to conquer from the eastern Adriatic to East Africa.

    d. only Germany was considered a serious long-term threat.

_____ **12.** Which of the following describes the Battle of Midway?

   a. Admiral Yamamoto wanted to force U.S. defenses back to the California coast.

   b. Armed ships faced one another directly instead of using planes and bombers.

   c. The Japanese navy was concentrated near the location of the battle.

   d. The United States lost several aircraft carriers in the victory.

_____ **13.** Wartime migration caused the worst incident of racial violence in

   a. Los Angeles, California.   **c.** Detroit, Michigan.

   b. Washington, D.C.   **d.** Poston, Arizona.

_____ **14.** Japanese Americans generally faced more restrictions than Italian or German Americans during World War II because they

   a. held more political power in the United States.

   b. greatly outnumbered other immigrant groups.

   c. were more isolated from other Americans.

   d. lived along the West Coast.

_____ **15.** Why did Stalin want the Allies to open a second front in France?

   a. He wanted Germany to divide its troops between two fronts.

   b. Soviet forces were losing ground in Eastern Europe and in the South.

   c. He believed the Western Front was more important.

   d. His advisers told him the German U-boat presence in the English Channel was dangerous.

_____ **16.** President Truman's chief priority in using the atomic bomb was to

   a. become a superpower.   **c.** prepare for a U.S. invasion of Japan.

   b. save American lives.   **d.** protect the lives of Japanese civilians.

_____ **17.** Which group did Nazi ideology consider superior to other people?

   a. Zionists   **c.** Jehovah's Witnesses

   b. Gypsies   **d.** Aryans

_____ **18.** At the 1942 Wannsee Conference, Reinhard Heydrich

   a. decided to invade large territories that were home to millions of Jews.

   b. planned to carry out bogus medical experiments on prisoners.

   c. determined the need to build additional concentration camps.

   d. outlined a plan to exterminate about 11,000,000 Jews.

> "... disregard and contempt for human rights have resulted in barbarous acts which have outraged the conscience of mankind, and the advent [beginning] of a world in which human beings shall enjoy freedom of speech and belief and freedom from fear and want has been proclaimed as the highest aspiration [aim] of the common people, ...
>
> —*Universal Declaration of Human Rights, 1948*

Name _____ Class _____ Date _____

Directions: *Use the quotation on the previous page to answer question 19.*

_____ 19. What does this quotation from the Universal Declaration of Human Rights proclaim?
  a. The conscience of mankind wants to begin a new country.
  b. People should try to ensure freedom and happiness for all humans.
  c. Barbarous acts will never happen on Earth again.
  d. People should work toward becoming wealthy.

_____ 20. What is one result of World War II?
  a. Britain, France, and Spain began to seek new territories.
  b. General Douglas MacArthur supervised the rebuilding of Germany.
  c. Colonial peoples renewed their drive for independence from European powers.
  d. The United States had the world's largest military force.

C. Document-Based Assessment

Directions: *Use the poster below and your knowledge of social studies to answer question 21 on a separate sheet of paper. (10 points)*

Illinois Digital Archives/Illinois State Library

21. Interpret Images Why would the U.S. government have distributed a poster like this around the United States?

D. Critical Thinking

Directions: *Answer the following questions on a separate sheet of paper. (10 points each)*

22. Understand Sequence Describe the sequence of events that led to the U.S. development of the atomic bomb.

23. Compare and Contrast Why was the United States considered a stronger superpower than the Soviet Union following World War II?

Answer Key

Vocabulary Builder

Student answers should demonstrate understanding of the vocabulary.

Reading Strategy

1. the Soviet Army reached the Oder River
2. also
3. less than one month

Enrichment

Student projects should demonstrate research, creative thinking, and appropriate presentation. Use *Assessment Rubrics* to evaluate the project.

Geography and History
North Africa

1. The desert that covers much of North Africa would have presented a challenge for the American armed forces.
2. The Allied forces in the 1942 offensive from Casablanca, Morocco to Tunisia would have first had to cross mountains. After that, they would have had to travel across the northern part of the Sahara.
3. Possible response: By moving their courses farther south, the Allied offensives would have traveled farther into the heart of the Sahara. There, they may have encountered even more dangers and difficult terrain that included tall mountain peaks.

Biography
Navajo Code Talkers

1. They came together and identified approximately 200 common Navajo terms that could be related to important military terms. They also devised a method of transmitting nonmilitary terms.

2. Their contributions went unrecognized because the code was so valuable that the government kept the code classified until 1968. This prevented the public from learning about the work of the code talkers.
3. Possible response: The Japanese code breakers were mostly trained in English. Without knowledge of the Navajo language, they would have been unable to determine the English meanings of the Navajo terms used in order to decipher the code.

Landmark Decisions of the Supreme Court

1. Possible answer: Judge Black argues that the order was based on a need to secure the West Coast of the United States, not on prejudice.
2. Possible answer: Judge Murphy disagrees with the decision because he thinks the decision is based on race rather than on substantial information.

Biography
Ira Hayes (1923–1955)

1. Hayes was born on the Pima Reservation in Arizona and had barely left the reservation before he enlisted in the United States Marines.
2. The soldiers raised the American flag at the top of Mount Suribachi on Iwo Jima.
3. Possible response: Hayes may have suggested that he did not feel like a hero because so many of his fellow soldiers lost their lives in the fighting on Iwo Jima. He might have wished the photo had never been taken because it brought him attention and recognition that he did not want.

Answer Key

Biography
The Marines at Iwo Jima

1. The Japanese troops had entrenched themselves in the mountainsides and built tunnels around the island, which made it difficult for American forces to counterattack.
2. The photograph captures the raising of the American flag atop Mount Suribachi on February 23, 1945.
3. Iwo Jima provided the U.S. forces in the Pacific with a location from which they could launch air attacks against Japan. The island also offered a place for damaged planes to land when returning from aerial attacks.

Link to Literature
Night

1. He carries heavy stone blocks for 12 hours a day.
2. Wiesel states that anyone that the Nazis determine to be too weak for work will be killed. Wiesel is concerned about his father because he thinks that his father has aged a great deal.
3. Wiesel implies the men have been strong enough both mentally and physically to survive. Their shared experiences seem to have created a bond between the survivors.

History Comics
Postwar Goals

Possible answer: Stalin, Roosevelt, and Churchill met in Yalta in February, 1945.

Possible answer: Roosevelt and Churchill wanted free elections but Stalin was reluctant to agree.

Possible answer: Roosevelt and Churchill accepted Stalin's promises, not knowing that he would later fail to keep them.

Possible response: People in Poland may have been happy because they would be able to vote for their leaders. People in Germany may have been angry that their country would be divided. People in both countries may have been upset because they were not represented at the conferences.

Section 1 Quiz

1. d   2. b   3. e   4. c   5. a
6. f   7. b   8. d   9. a   10. d

Section 2 Quiz

1. g   2. b   3. h   4. d   5. c
6. a   7. b   8. d   9. c   10. c

Section 3 Quiz

1. Harry S. Truman
2. Manhattan Project
3. Albert Einstein
4. D-Day
5. island hopping
6. Battle of the Bulge
7. c   8. a   9. d   10. b

Section 4 Quiz

1. Nazi attempt to kill all Jews, as well as other "undesirables," under their control
2. laws Hitler instituted that denied German citizenship to Jews, prohibited marriage between Jews and non-Jews, and segregated Jews in German society
3. attack by German troops on Jewish synagogues and businesses in which many Jews were arrested, injured, and killed
4. willful annihilation of a racial, political, or cultural group
5. a place where members of specially designated groups are confined

Answer Key

6. U.S. organization that worked with the Red Cross to save thousands of Eastern European Jews

7. b   8. c   9. b   10. d

Section 5 Quiz

1. e   2. f   3. b   4. c   5. g
6. d   7. d   8. b   9. c   10. b

Test A

1. j   2. f   3. d   4. c   5. h
6. g   7. b   8. i   9. a   10. e
11. a   12. c   13. a   14. b   15. c
16. c   17. b   18. c   19. a   20. b

21. Possible answers: The image encourages people to ration food so that soldiers in World War II will have enough to eat and drink. The poster encourages people because it doesn't say "do without," it says "do with less," which means that people do not need to starve themselves to help the troops. Also, the man in the image appears thankful, so the poster shows that soldiers appreciate the sacrifice that other Americans are making.

22. The Allies' unified strategy for winning the war was to first gain victory in Europe and then focus on the war in the Pacific. Stalin, Churchill, and Roosevelt agreed that Hitler was the greatest threat so they concentrated their efforts on Germany. The nations of the Axis Powers each had individual goals in the war and thus never shared a coordinated strategy for defeating the Allies. Hitler wanted to dominate Europe, Mussolini wanted an Italian Empire, and Tojo sought Japanese control of the Western Pacific and Asia.

23. During the war, many women found jobs in areas that fell outside the traditional realm of women's work, such as manufacturing and heavy industry. Women also worked in white-collar jobs such as secretarial or clerical work. Life changed for African Americans because

leaders such as A. Philip Randolph fought to end African Americans' status as second-class citizens. Roosevelt issued Executive Order 8802 that ensured fair hiring practices in jobs funded with government money and a committee to enforce these requirements.

Test B

1. i   2. k   3. d   4. m   5. b
6. f   7. c   8. j   9. h   10. l
11. d   12. a   13. c   14. c   15. a
16. b   17. d   18. d   19. b   20. c

21. The U.S. government wanted to encourage people to support the war effort through rationing. Rationing and many other regulations were unpopular, so the government would have wanted to encourage people by showing them the way that rationing benefits the armed forces.

22. By 1920, scientists began researching the idea of producing an atomic bomb. At the beginning of World War II, Albert Einstein signed a letter to President Roosevelt urging him to proceed with atomic development. In 1942, Roosevelt established the Manhattan Project to develop an atomic bomb. A number of prominent scientists worked in Los Alamos, New Mexico, to construct the weapon. Other scientists and engineers worked on aspects of the project without being aware of their real work. The first weapon test was in July 1945.

23. Except for the attack on Pearl Harbor, no major battles had been fought on American soil, and U.S. industry had also grown considerably during the war. The nation was wealthy and had a powerful military. On the other hand, the people, cities, and industries of the Soviet Union had suffered significantly. Even though the Soviet Union had the world's largest military at the time, the United States developed the atomic bomb.

CURRICULUM